For a Palestinian

Bilal Hasna & Aaron Kilercioglu

T0179944

methuen | drama

LONDON • NEW YORK • OXFORD • NEW DELHI • SYDNEY

METHUEN DRAMA
Bloomsbury Publishing Plc
50 Bedford Square, London, WC1B 3DP, UK
1385 Broadway, New York, NY 10018, USA
29 Earlsfort Terrace, Dublin 2, Ireland

BLOOMSBURY, METHUEN DRAMA and the Methuen
Drama logo are trademarks of Bloomsbury Publishing Plc

First published in Great Britain 2022

A catalogue record for this book is available from the British Library.

Library of Congress Control Number: 2022944268

ISBN: PB: 978-1-3503-6887-3
ePDF: 978-1-3503-6888-0
eBook: 978-1-3503-6889-7

Series: Modern Plays

Typeset by Mark Heslington Ltd, Scarborough, North Yorkshire

To find out more about our authors and books visit
www.bloomsbury.com and sign up for our newsletters.

WoLab presents. . .

For a Palestinian

By Bilal Hasna and Aaron Kilercioglu

Co-writers **Bilal Hasna** and **Aaron Kilercioglu**
Director **Aaron Kilercioglu**
Performer **Bilal Hasna**
Sound Designer **Holly Khan**
Lighting Designer **Ros Chase**
Set Designer **Jida Akil**
Graphic Design by **CIWA Design**
PR by **Caitlin Plimmer** for **Chloé Nelkin Consulting**

For WoLab:

Creative Director **Alistair Wilkinson**
Associate Director **Kaleya Baxe**

With thanks to: Alia Alzougbi, Eliza Bacon, Rikki Beadle-Blair, Bristol Old Vic, Bristol Palestine Museum and Cultural Centre, Camden People's Theatre, Isabelle Clarke, Eliot Cohen, Billie Collins, Sue Emmas, Hani Hasna, Marwan Hasna, and the whole Hasna family, Hannah Kumari, Ben Jamal, Jerwood Space, Na'amod, Roua Naboulsi, National Youth Theatre of Great Britain, New Diorama Theatre, P21 Gallery, Palestine Solidarity Campaign, Ruari Paterson-Achenbach, Issy Snape, Punchdrunk, Harry Redding, RTYDS, Holly Adomah Thompson, Lyndsey Turner, the WoLab extended family, Yahya Zaloom.

This production was first performed at Camden People's Theatre on 13 September 2022, before transferring to Bristol Old Vic on 13 October 2022.

Foreword

As I write this Israel has just begun its latest bombardment of Gaza. It has killed, within its first hour, eight Palestinians, including a five-year-old girl. There is a line in this play which speaks to the story being played out right now, the story played out so many times before: 'What do Palestinians do,' the narrator asks, 'except vanish, in one way or another?'

At the heart of this important play are two stories: that of Wa'el Zuaiter, a Palestinan who founded the Italian Committee in Support of the Palestinian People, and that of Bilal, as a British Palestinian navigating the complexities of that identity. It is a tale of a beautiful love story between a man and a woman. It is a story of the transcendent love of a people for their homeland.

Mahmoud Darwish, the National Poet of Palestine, once wrote that Palestinians, like everyone else, want to live ordinary lives, but that when a person is deprived of their homeland, they are obliged to become a slave to that homeland. This play navigates the complex pathways of that enslavement and how it impacts upon ordinary lives. The play speaks to the truth that lies at the heart of solidarity: that solidarity is an act of empathy, an act of love which recognises the humanity in a people suffering injustice and shares in that humanity. A recognition that, once achieved, drives one to act.

The play speaks to me as someone who runs a solidarity organisation and as a British Palestinian, who, like Bilal, was not born in Palestine, does not speak Arabic, and has had to find his own answers to the question of what it means to be both British and a Palestinian. It is an emotional journey which the play exposes beautifully when the narrator says '. . . there's this feeling. And it really is impossible to translate. But if you feel it, you know what it is. If you're watching this and you're Palestinian, you know what it is.'

But this play speaks far more universally. It deserves to be read and seen not least because it tells the story of a man, Wa'el Zuaiter, who needs to be remembered for so much more than his death. Not because his was a life filled with extraordinary acts but because his was a life, as portrayed, filled with ordinary and beautiful acts of love, including his unyielding love for Palestine.

This play in turn is an act of love. For a Palestinian. For Palestine. For everyone who retains the hope that is also at the heart of solidarity activism, a hope in the capacity of human beings to do good.

Ben Jamal
Director, Palestine Solidarity Campaign

Friday 5 August, 2022

Jida Akil – Set Designer

Jida Akil is a Syrian/Lebanese Set & Costume Designer based in London. She graduated from Central Saint Martins in 2021 and has since been working with notable theatres such as the Young Vic as the Jerwood Assistant Designer as well as designing for acclaimed companies such as Complicité. Her designs have also been selected for exhibitions with the Prague Quadrennial and World Stage Design.

Recent credits include: *The Poison Belt* (Jermyn Street Theatre); *Ruckus* (Summerhall, Edinburgh, and Southwark Playhouse); *Painkiller* (Theatre Royal Stratford East); *Trump L'Oeil* (Upstairs At The Gatehouse); *Give Me The Sun* (Blue Elephant Theatre); *Funeral Flowers* (UK Tour); *Heavy Weather* (Fourth Monkey Training Company); *The 4th Country* (Park Theatre); *Darling* (The Hope Theatre); *Complicité do A-Level Drama* (Complicité, UK Schools Tour); *Haramacy* (The Albany Deptford); *Solus, Just Another Soup Can, Out!* (all Platform Theatre); and *Through The Arches* (Central School of Ballet).

Recent Assistant/Associate credits include: *Middle* (National Theatre); *The Collaboration, Hamlet* (all Young Vic); *L'Orfeo* (Weiner Staatsoper); and *My Son's A Queer But What Can You Do?* (Turbine Theatre).

Ros Chase – Lighting Designer

Ros Chase (she/her) is a London-based Lighting Designer. She is currently studying at Guildhall School on the Theatre Technology course alongside her professional work at venues including the Phoenix Theatre, Southwark Playhouse and Leeds Playhouse. Ros thrives off the theatre environment and giving creative input towards a show. She is passionate about using theatre and the arts as a form of education, inspiration and inclusivity. She enjoys exploring how creative disciplines can transform the atmosphere and aid the delivery of a story, captivating the audience and making it accessible to all. Ros is especially interested in theatre that amplifies the voices of underrepresented communities, specifically women and members of the LGBTQ+ community. Ros' designs have been described as 'vivid and symbolic', using colour and intensity as a subtle way to portray messages.

Holly Khan – Sound Designer

Holly Khan is a British/Guyanese composer, sound designer and multi-instrumentalist. Holly champions the notion art is for all and continually seeks ways of bringing art into the community. Highlights include musical direction for *Amal Meets Alice* with The Story Museum and Good Chance Theatre, sound design for *It's About Time* for UN Women and Battersea Arts Centre, composition for *Their Voices*, featured at the Barbican. Holly's compositions have featured at the Royal Albert Hall, South Bank Centre, Oxford Playhouse, Mercury Colchester, The Sage Newcastle and Summerhall Edinburgh.

Bilal Hasna – Co-writer and Performer

Bilal is a British, Palestinian and Pakistani actor and writer from London. Over the last two years he has worked on projects with the BBC, Channel 4, Netflix and Warner Bros., and has just finished filming a starring role in the upcoming Disney+ series *Extraordinary*. *For a Palestinian* is his professional writing debut. He hopes, with all of his heart, to see a free Palestine in his lifetime.

Aaron Kilercioglu – Co-writer and Director

Aaron is a theatre- and film maker. Raised in Vienna by Turkish and Canadian parents, he has recently written plays about diasporic identity formation, Middle Eastern politics, and how fungi might just be the key to saving our world. He is the winner of BOLD Playwrights and the Methuen Drama

'Other' Prize, and was shortlisted for the Theatre503 International Playwriting Prize. His short films have been screened in festivals across the world. He also translates between English, German and Turkish. He lives in South London.

Alistair Wilkinson – Producer and Creative Director of WoLab

Alistair is a highly experienced, award-winning, queer, working class and disabled artist, originally from Manchester, now living in East London. They trained at Royal Central School of Speech and Drama, as well as on the Royal Court's Invitation Writers Group, and also completed an MA at RADA/Birkbeck. In the past they have made work for organisations such as the BBC, Sky Arts, the National Theatre, The Old Vic, Barbican Centre, Shoreditch Town Hall, Arcola Theatre and Curious Monkey, amongst many others. A lot of Alistair's work focuses on themes of grief, sickness, intimacy and intoxication. They are the former Head of Artist Development at The Old Vic; and are currently leading on all talent development at Punchdrunk, working in the UK, internationally and digitally. They are an Associate Artist at the National Youth Theatre, a Connect Artist for RTYDS, a Trustee for Boundless and a Script Reader for the Bush Theatre, Theatre Uncut and The Papatango Prize. Alistair is the Founder and Creative Director of WoLab, and to date, they have raised over £1.77m in funding for various artistic projects.

Bristol Old Vic

Bristol Old Vic is the longest continuously running theatre in the UK and celebrated its 250th anniversary in 2016. The historic playhouse aims to inspire audiences with its own original productions, both at home and on tour, whilst nurturing the next generation of artists, whether that be through their 350-strong Young Company, their many outreach and education projects or their trailblazing artist development programme, Bristol Ferment. They prioritise their public funding to support experiment and innovation, to allow access to their programme for people who would not otherwise encounter it, or be able to afford it, and to keep their extraordinary heritage alive and animated.

Bristol Old Vic's 2018 redevelopment transformed its front of house into a warm and welcoming space for all of Bristol to enjoy, created a new studio theatre and opened up its unique theatrical heritage to the public for the first time. Since the March 2020 lockdown, the theatre completely reimagined a digital version of itself, experimented with streamed performances available globally, maintained links with their most vulnerable participants and welcomed live audiences during the moments when restrictions were lifted. Now, once again, Bristol Old Vic is thrilled to be able to throw open its doors and welcome back audiences both physically and digitally as it looks towards the future.

Camden People's Theatre

Founded twenty-eight years ago, Camden People's Theatre is one of Britain's most influential studio theatres. Its mission is to champion different ways of thinking about the world by supporting emerging artists making adventurous theatre – particularly about issues that matter to people now. Its work is rooted in the communities of Camden and London. Through it, they celebrate the bold, the spirited and the unconventional.

WoLab

WoLab is a working laboratory for artists to create. They provide performance makers of all experiences with the opportunity to have a go. WoLab trains, mentors, nurtures and creatively entitles artists, helping them discover and refine their talents, and then showcases those talents to the industry. Current work in development includes: *ENG-ER-LAND* by Hannah Kumari, touring to 30+ venues throughout Spring/Summer 2022; *For A Palestinian* by Bilal Hasna and Aaron Kilercioglu, returning to Camden People's Theatre in autumn 2022, before transferring to Bristol Old Vic; *Screwdriver* by Eve Cowley and Elin Schofield, recently workshopped with Sheffield Theatres and Sheffield Royal Society For the Blind, heading on tour in 2023; *A nightmare is witchwork* by Billie Collins; *In the Net* by Misha Levkov; *A Romantic Comedy* by Tiwa Lade; *TIGER* by Tom Kelsey; *Ostrich* by Alistair Wilkinson; and *The Director's Development Fund*, in partnership with Hannah Joss and Stage Director's UK. Past work includes: *RAINER* (Arcola Theatre – Off-West End Nominated); *First Commissions* (Paines Plough); *The Actor-Writer Programme* (Theatre N16/Bunker Theatre); *Man-Cub* (RADA/King's Head); *PlayList* (King's Head); *happy ever after?* (Bunker Theatre); and R&D's of *heavymetalsexyanimal* by Sam Rees (Theatre Deli); *Asperger's Children* by Peter Machen (Trinity Laban); and *We'll Be Who We Are* by Naomi Obeng.

For a Palestinian

'You have something in this world, so stand for it.'
— Ghassan Kanafani

'And it is the duty of the entire world to support only what is just; for only with the commitment of everyone will justice return.'
— Wa'el Adel Zuaiter

Notes:

Lines in italics indicate direct speech by a character other than Wa'el.

Stage directions are set in parentheses and italics.

A **RECORDING** *is either an interview with Bilal's family members, with co-writer Aaron, or found archival recordings, and plays as V.O.*

// indicates a change of some kind: place, space, time

A – indicates an interruption

. . . Indicates either a trailing off, a breather, a shift or a transition.

For Wa'el & Janet

and

Feya & Nada

(*The faint sound of radio static. It swells and morphs into a tapestry of sounds from the play: news recordings, interviews, opera, freedom chants.*)

(**Bilal** *enters. He takes in the audience. He's ready.*)

(*The soundscape continues to crescendo, louder and louder, and just before the climax – an email notification.* **Bilal** *checks his phone.*)

Bilal   The message arrives in my inbox at 5.57pm, on Wednesday 17 April, 2018.

'Dear Hani, Asma, Bilal and Iman,

It is with great pleasure that we invite you to Orcadia Halls, West Jerusalem, on the 8th September, to mark the wedding of Ahmed and Alaa Hasna.

We look forward to celebrating with you soon.

Kind regards,

Ahmed, Alaa, Amani, Sadeen, Mohammed, Fouad' –

Listen, it's a big family.

'Ali Senior, Ali Junior, Tahani, Kayed, Ibrahim, Nadia and Hussein.'

My cousin Ahmed's getting married!!

Am I on the verge of tears at the prospect of him flying the nest? Absolutely.

Have I met Ahmed less than five times? Sure. But listen, Dad's already on Skyscanner looking up flights, I mean, there's no question about it, we're going.

It's in our blood, us Arabs love a good love story.

It'll be the first time I go back to Palestine since 2011 . . . I was twelve then, and if I'm being honest I didn't really know what was going on. I was a bit naive. We're talking wearing a Hollister puffer jacket whilst posing with the peace sign next to the separation wall kind of naive.

But I'm nineteen now, about to go into my second year of uni. And I've learnt a bit more about my Palestinian heritage, like I know the history better. But I'm thinking, I've got five months until the wedding, I'm going to do my research. Become an expert. You know? Reconnect with my roots.

So I start. And I can't lie, it is Wikipedia articles and YouTube intro videos at first. But soon I'm reading whole books. And in the middle of this dry and quite complicated history of the *1001 Nights* . . .

I find the most amazing story.

//

(**Bilal** *becomes* **Wa'el**: *early thirties, gentle, polite, invitingly warm. When speaking English, he has a soft Palestinian accent.*)

Wa'el (*in Arabic*)   Where to begin?

(*Pause.*)

Is it okay for me to speak Arabic? Who here speaks Arabic? Put your hand up.

(*In English.*)

(*Depending on the amount of hands up in the audience:*)

Not too many of you. Okay, no problem. We can do English. It's good to be respectful.	Mashallah. Let's do this in English for those who don't. It's good to be respectful.

Where to begin?

Perhaps an introduction? My name is Wa'el Adel Zuaiter. I was born in Nablus, Palestine, in 1934, and since then I have never been able to stay still.

As a teenager, me and my friends spent summers cycling around Jaffa, swimming in the sea and soaking up the sweet smell of the orange groves . . .

I studied civil engineering in Baghdad.

Arab parents, what can I say?

Then Kuwait for work, later Germany, but it is in Rome that my life truly began.

When I arrive here in 1962, it feels like I am at the heart of culture: music, literature, movies! You can practically *smell* Fellini, *taste* Pavarotti and *hear* Puccini, while Sophia Loren could be waiting for you just around the corner.

There is history here, and you can feel it. Yani, it is not disputed, it is being made right now, out in the piazzas over espressos and red wine and –

And it is here, on an evening in July 1962, that the story begins.

//

Wa'el   I am in a gallery off the back of a luxury shopping street. Galleria Augusto Consorti.

My friend and housemate Salvatore has brought us here. Salvatore's shirt is always half-unbuttoned, his voice a bit too loud, but he knows where the best parties are.

Andiamo amico.

The space is packed to the brim with students and it is loud. The paintings are all suspended on strings from the ceiling, their backs facing each other, which visually looks great but practically is a nightmare, it –

(**Wa'el** *struggles to make his way through the crowd.*)

– it makes it almost impossible to move. So I am just standing here, sort of squashed between two paintings when –

(**Wa'el** *turns to see the painting. Pause. He's completely taken aback.*)

Questo? You like?

It's a watercolour of a small room.

There's a view out of French windows that looks onto Rome. Pale-pink curtains frame a small sofa in the centre of the room, with four pillows crumpled on it, two crimson and two midnight blue.

The colours are bright and vivid, and in the corner, on a dresser, there's a bowl of oranges which, once you notice, make the whole painting . . . orange.

Yes. I like.

As I look back at him, Salvatore has already walked off to join another group –

What do you like about it?

(**Wa'el** *looks around, confused.*)

Me?

Yes!

The voice is coming from behind the painting.

I look down and all I can see is the end of a yellow dress and a pair of sandals, with feet turned into each other.

Well, come on . . . what do you like?

Um. Sorry it feels like I'm talking to the painting!

Yeah this back-to-back painting set-up, it's visually great, but with this many people it's pr –

Practically a nightmare!

Exactly!

(*Beat.*)

What do you see?

Oh you're beautiful. Masterful use of colour. Innovative perspective. You were probably painted by the world's greatest artist.

Who painted it?

Me.

Really?

Yeah. And the one you're looking at.

Oh.

So, what do you think? I'm trying to develop so I'd appreciate an honest –

Orange.

You think it's orange?

Yes . . . I – I like orange!

There's not a lot of orange in that painting.

It reminds me of the sea.

Orange reminds you of the sea?

No – yes – um, the sea at home. Jaffa? It is famous for its orange trees. The beach is always covered in orange peel.

Oh right. I also grew up by the sea.

Really?

Yeah, but mine was blue. Sydney.

We always find each other.

Who?

People of the sea.

(*Beat.*)

I see the sandals turn in another direction. I think someone has tapped her on the shoulder, trying to get her attention –

My name is Wa'el.

Janet, she says, *it was nice to meet you Wael*, and then she turns and walks away . . .

//

Wa'el   Later that evening, the image of a bright orange imprinted on my mind, we return home.

Home is Number 19 Via del Mario de Fiori, but we know it as: Mariuccia's Pensione.

Mariuccia is seventy-nine years old and wearing every single one of those years on her sleeve. She is beautiful in the way only life can make you.

Guiali, vino?

Mariuccia loves throwing big dinners for us and watching from the sidelines. Tonight she has made home-made ravioli, grilled bream, fresh caprese, all washed down with warm Chianti!

All of us here are foreigners, far from our homes – well, Salvatore's technically not a foreigner, but he's from Sardinia, so he might as well be from a different continent, or as he would often say:

I might as well be an Arab.

You might as well be, I would often reply.

Then there's Cori. British aristocracy. In Rome for 'personal development' paid for by the parents . . . But he owns good records and buys nice wine so we keep him around.

Has anyone heard about Leila's friend Amir?

Not my friend – my lover!

That's Leila, the French translator, the real Bohemian amongst us. We are working together on an Italian translation of the *1001 Nights* directly from the original Arabic!

You British never say what you mean.

Dinner here is always a bustle of half-understood, highly pretentious conversations. And usually I'm right in the middle of it all but tonight . . .

You know when everything just feels like a distraction?

Well whatever Amir is to you, I've heard he's gone off to Algeria.

Algeria?

The fever of independence. The chap's gone absolutely mad with it. He's going to fight every last Frenchman until they leave.

He will be slaughtered, amico!

Well it's his own fault, isn't it?

This nationalism in the Arab countries. C'est juvénile, non?

Juvenile?

Mais oui! We saw it in Europe . . . it doesn't end well, c'est stupide la.

It's his home.

Home! There is no such thing anymore. It is 1963, Wa'el, not 1914.

He's protecting his home. I don't think that is juvenile.

But going to fight, amico? He will kill people!

The French will kill his family.

The Algerians should be peaceful like every other colony. I mean, look at the Indians, Gandhi. A civilised discussion led to their independence, not this militancy. I can't believe your chap Amir buys into this death-riddled hatred.

It's not about hate . . . it's . . .

It's love. He loves Algeria. He wants his people to be in charge of –

Come on, do you really believe in love? It's a bit parochial, non? Love . . . c'est une construct. It is a way for the man to subjugate the woman. A way for countries to manipulate its people!

What is there to live for if not love?

Wa'el the romantic!

Have you ever been in love, amico?

Not yet, bas I will be!

He will be! How can you be so sure chap?

Mariuccia, est-ce-que tu crois? Is love real?

Mariuccia's in the corner smiling to herself.

(**Mariuccia** *laughs to herself.*)

Exactement! Love is bullshit!

Dio mio giovanni, I have loved . . .

Précisément, dit-leurs! Love is a political mechanism, non?

No, no, no, no. It's all love. It's always love. Si?

//

Bilal The more I learn about Wa'el's life, the more curious I get. But there's not that much information online.

(**Bilal** *retrieves a sound recorder.*)

Like, even my dad who knows *everything* about Palestine doesn't have a clue who this guy is.

(**Bilal** *clicks play on the recorder.*)

RECORDING:

Hani   I don't know about him, I've never heard of him. What's his name? Wa'el what?

Bilal Zuaiter.

Hani Zuaiter?

Bilal Yeah.

Hani ZOO-AITER. Wa'el Zoo-aiter.

Bilal Yeah, is that how you pronounce it?

And I start feeling like a proper detective, finding bits about his life on the internet.

Hani You should talk to Amo Marwaan, he might know more.

And as I'm searching I start finding resemblances with myself?

Marwan Hello Bilal, how are you?

I mean, sure, maybe these parallels are a bit far-fetched, but like . . . we're both Palestinians living in the West.

And Wa'el has a sister . . . I mean *same*.

Bilal I just had a few questions, Amo Marwaan.

Or the fact that Wa'el was creating the first Italian translation of the *1001 Nights* . . . and I've *read* the *1001 Nights*.

Listen, we're like connected.

//

Wa'el For a week I cannot stop thinking about Janet and her sandals.

It's funny, thinking of someone without knowing their face, so it's just a voice, a sound. And it is always accompanied by the image of a single bright orange.

I'm sitting at the kitchen table fumbling with letters from my family. Mariuccia is kneading dough by the counter and

Salvatore is peeling carrots for her. Cori is doing what he does best: eavesdropping.

Good letters, amico?

Everyone at home is very excited about a new group – the PLO.

What, your family is into armed resistance?

Cori – . . . Salvatore can I . . . I have a question for you.

Si, amico.

In the gallery . . . in the gallery I met someone, her name was Janet.

You like her?

No! I mean she's nice. I like her art. I would like to see her art again.

Her art, amico . . .?

Yes. Her art. She's talented. Do you know where she works?

No. You coming to party?

No, no you go ahead.

Ciao amico. Cori, you finish the carrots for me, si?

Why can't Wa'el finish them?

I need to go meet Leila!

Leila and I meet twice a week at Cafe Agua, with its famously loud grandfather clock. Over a bottle of wine and a few espressos we spend the afternoon working through my enormous manuscript of the *Nights*.

Translation is never just swapping an Arabic word for an Italian one. You can do better Wa'el.

Okay, he is . . . shu ismo? Yani, he is going into the water.

Is he going? Or is he stumbling? Or venturing? attacking?

Um . . . maybe he –

Is he falling, tripping, diving, advancing, travelling?

Yes, I understand –

We are creating a representation. So it matters. Every sentence, every time we choose falling instead of advancing, smack instead of touch, angry instead of upset. It matters.

I come home exhausted, stumbling, falling, venturing into bed, thinking I have successfully distracted myself for the day until, as soon as I shut my eyes, I see orange and I smell orange. All night.

(**Wa'el** *falls asleep.*)

//

(**Wa'el** *wakes up to the sound of music.*)

Vino, guaili?

Our usual Thursday dinner. Mariuccia has set up a real spread: lasagne, smoked fish, salad.

This looks delicieuse Mariuccia!

(*The sound of the doorbell.*)

Ah it must be my friend.

What friend?

Just a friend.

(*To the room.*)

What do you want to bet it is some beautiful young woman?

And Leila is right. She is stunning: dressed in wide green flared trousers, an orange blazer and white blouse. Home-made jewellery hangs from her neck and her ears.

Tutti, this my friend. Janet.

Hi. Thanks for inviting me.

(*Pause.* **Wa'el** *can't really speak.*)

It can't be.

Janet sits across from me.

She really is . . .

And her eyes?

I mean, how is it possible that just by looking at some people your stomach goes warm?

(*Whispering.*) I thought you didn't know her!

Oh amico you mean this Janet? Janet, mi amico loves your art.

Oh yeah?

Erm . . . yes. It is beautiful.

Where did you see it?

Galleria Augustino.

Oh yeah . . .

Janet has an exhibition tomorrow tesoro, we must all go.

If I can set it all up on time.

What do you mean?

I've gotta carry everything tomorrow morning because someone decided to cancel at the last minute.

I had to! It is an emergency!

How is taking that American exchange student around town an emergency?

She's single! And leaves on Friday . . .

Erm . . . I can help. If you want help?

Guaili very strong man.

Your voice . . .

Me?

Yes. You're . . . orange? Oranges by the sea?

Yes.

I knew it was you.

(Beat.)

Do you know each other?

Well we've never seen each other. Only heard.

How romantic, non?

He's a lot more handsome than I thought he'd be.

Oh look! Our darling Wa'el's gone all red!

You're very beautiful too.

I'd love your help with the paintings tomorrow. If you have the time.

RECORDING:

Hani   And then what happened?

(Whilst the recording plays, **Wa'el** *gleefully enacts the moments* **Bilal** *is describing.)*

RECORDING:

Bilal   Well the next day, he really did carry the paintings to the gallery that Janet was having her exhibition at. And yeah he spent the whole day there, because she had promised to take him to dinner afterwards. So he just looked around the gallery – he just loved the work I think. But basically –

Hani   And what did they do after the exhibition?

Bilal   Um, after they finished taking down the stuff I guess they must have gone for dinner together, she took him for dinner. Which I think is pretty cool for the 60s, I mean, did a woman ever take you for dinner back then?

Hani   I'm not that old – I was born in 1963.

Bilal   Okay but you know what I mean . . . and they loved to go to the pictures, and like, I don't know, sooner or later they fell in love.

And the next four years was basically like a storybook romance. I mean they cooked for each other, they wrote letters to each other even though they lived like a ten-minute walk from each other, which I think is really cute. They went to dinner parties, they hosted their own dinner parties, Mariuccia obviously helped. Um . . . what else?

Oh! He actually took singing lessons for two years, he took opera singing lessons in Rome.

Hani   Opera lessons? Why?

Bilal   Because he loved opera remember! And most importantly he continued his translation work on the *1001 Nights*, he kept going for all those years – with Leila, obviously, who worked him really hard. And Janet continued to paint and in those years she gained quite a big following. And they went dancing, and she loved jazz, and he loved opera. But they loved to dance together. And they built a life together, in Rome!

But then . . . yeah, obviously 1967 came along.

//

Wa'el   May 1967. Tensions in the Middle East are rising. The Israelis and the Egyptians are on the brink of something and we all hope it's not war.

Janet and I are sharing a bottle of Chianti.

Okay let me just get this straight. You have no combat training, no real knowledge of war, or what it entails?

Correct.

You have no military contacts, no idea how one even joins an army –

Yes.

And you're planning to drive across five countries and two continents to fight over 200,000 Israeli troops?

I've told her that if war does break out I want to go back. A Palestinian friend has agreed to drive us there in his Fiat.

You actually want to go fight?

I can't sit here drinking wine while listening to reports about my friends and family being shot!

Wa'el, you can't kill a spider.

It's my home –

Last week I watched you spend two hours trying to usher the ants out of my kitchen without killing them.

Janet –

So please, tell me, how are you going to shoot a gun?

(*Pause.*)

You've got nothing to prove.

I'm not trying to –

You're just as Palestinian here. At home.

Palestine is home.

(*Pause.*)

You could die if you go.

Something will die if I don't.

'Something'?

Yes.

Right, well please forgive me for not wanting to lose my partner over an abstract noun.

I don't know how to translate this feeling for you Janet.

I need you to try.

(*Pause.*)

Every evening that week we sit in Janet's apartment listening to the news. Until finally –

RECORDING:

Associated Press   'The tension in the Middle East over the Gulf of Aqaba blockade develops into full-scale war.'

June 5th 1967.

I decide to leave Rome that same night.

The journey should take us a week, through Yugoslavia, Bulgaria, Turkey, Lebanon, only stopping to rest.

Just promise you'll come back.

I promise.

(*Beat.*)

Alright.

It is 3am on June 5th when we start our journey.

//

(*Luton Airport. Flight announcements over the tannoy.*)

Bilal   It's 3am in Luton and it's pissing it down. My dad always books the 4am Easyjet flight because it's 10 quid cheaper.

I've only slept two hours and to make a bad situation worse? They've gotten rid of the Burger King. How am I going to get through this without my vegan double whopper, no cheese, extra onion?

As usual, we're running late and my mum's in Duty Free deciding whether the aunties would prefer face cream or hand cream.

Mum! Come on!

She gets both.

We just about make it to the gate, but in true Arab style we've delayed the flight by ten minutes because it turns out you actually can't take seven Duty Free bags on the plane. Thanks Mum.

So once we've stuffed our XL Toblerone bars in our hand luggage, the flight finally departs.

//

(**Wa'el** *sat in a car. Faint music plays over the radio.*)

Wa'el   It is funny, crossing from West to East.

I wish I could tell you it is dramatic changes. I wish I could tell you it is a mosaic of culture. But mostly it is long streets. Mostly it is looking out the window at the passing trees. Mostly it is people being people the way people are people all across the world.

My friend, he does most of the driving. It is a silent journey apart from the sound of the radio.

(**Wa'el** *fiddles with the radio and falls asleep. Radio static turns into a recording.*)

RECORDING:

Bilal   If it's okay, I'd like to talk about the '67 war.

(*. . . radio static, channels switching. . .*)

Marwaan   It was the second time in my life I saw a dead body. We thought about leaving bas Shido Ali stood in front of all of us [. . .] and he said 'no one will leave this house ever'. And he said 'if they are going to kill us, let them come and kill us here, in the house. But we are not going to leave anywhere' I was so afraid that I got to sleep so that I don't hear anything or know anything. If I'm going to die I want to die whilst sleeping.

Bilal?

Bilal   Yes, I'm still here.

(. . . *radio static, channels switching* . . .**Wa'el** *wakes up.*)

Wa'el   It's June 10th and we have travelled 3,167 kilometres in the Fiat 125. We are by the coast in Beirut, only about three hours to the border to Palestine.

Five cars have stopped in the middle of the road. We turn the bend, and another four cars are there, not moving. Two people are sat in the front of a car, hugging each other. Shufi mafi?

My friend stops the car.

Everyone has stopped their cars. People are stepping out. More and more people. Just standing on the road. Hugging each other.

They all say the same thing: Halas. Halas. It's over.

RECORDING:

Bilal   If I were to ask you the question why was the 1967 war significant for Palestine, what would your answer be?

Hani   My answer would be because it was the nail in the coffin of Palestine. The final nail in the coffin of Palestine. We lost the last 22 per cent. They'd taken 78 cent in '48, left us with 22 per cent and then in 1967 we lost that 22 per cent.

The sea is reflecting the strong afternoon sun. It is high tide. I can hear the water from where we are parked.

(*Radio static, which turns into a news recording.*)

RECORDING:

Associated Press   Israel's victory was won by herself, alone and unaided.

(*Pause.*)

The war has ended before I have even arrived. I am late.

There is officially no more Palestine.

RECORDING:

Marwaan Uh, in general, I think it destroyed our . . . it destroyed our souls. Yani, we were completely – what they call it – completely lost. Completely lost.

//

(*Janet's apartment.*)

I've never seen you with a beard.

Does it suit me?

No.

(*They chuckle softly. They hug.*)

I didn't get to kill any spiders.

Not even an ant?

Not even an ant.

(*Laughter.*

Silence. Tears.)

It's gone.

I know.

(**Wa'el** *breaks down as the recording plays.*)

RECORDING:

Hani And what – he just came back to Italy straight away?

Bilal   Yeah from what I gather . . . we don't know exactly how long he was away for, but he definitely came back pretty soon after

Hani   And went straight to Janet's?

Bilal   Yeah, he only lived –

Hani   Did she know he was alive?

Bilal   I don't know, I wish I knew what they said to each other. But all his friends said that when he came back he was a changed person, like he had a new purpose in life.

//

Wa'el   I help Palestine in the only way I know: speaking to people.

The students at the universities. The waiters at the coffee shops. The taxi drivers, the shopkeepers. We speak to anyone who will listen.

We start holding meetings in Mariuccia's apartment every Thursday.

Here? In the living room? Well, we must help you get set up, non? On y va!

And the people come. One by one they ring the doorbell and I welcome them into our home.

(The doorbell rings with each new attendee.)

What was Israel to do? It's self-defence.

All land is stolen.

Have you got any more hummus?

I teach the people who come about the Nakba, and the Naksa, and everything in between.

I show them pictures of my home that is no longer my home. Pictures of the refugees, of my family.

And people start listening. More and more people are arriving to the meetings and soon we need a second, and then a third meeting a week to accommodate them all.

By the end of 1967 we form the Italian Committee in Support of the Palestinian People. A committee full of trade union leaders, feminists, students.

(**Wa'el** *starts physically creating the centre: hanging up posters, pamphlets, articles and Palestinian flags.*)

The living room is no longer enough so we pool our resources and open our own space across the street.

We spend an entire Sunday painting the walls.

We hang up maps and leaflets and letters and art that is donated to us. There are chairs and desks! And Mariuccia provides us with tea and food and –

It isn't anything special, but it's ours.

An actual office. All in solidarity of the Palestinian people.

Open four days a week. Which – for Italy – is actually quite a lot.

The movement is real, even Leila understands we don't have time for translating stories – there's actual work to do.

Everyone from Maricuccia's Pensione comes to the meetings to help and –

Well, not Cori, but that I don't mind so much. The British have a way of vanishing that us Arabs are used to by now. We just prefer when they don't reappear.

But no-one is more committed than Janet.

She comes to every Committee meeting. And she wears the keffiyeh around her shoulders like a shawl. And she laughs, and smiles, and she makes it make sense to the Italians.

The violence the Israelis are showing is completely disproportionate.

Don't they have a right to defend themselves?

Of course they do but if I throw a water balloon at the back of your head and then you turn around and shoot me in the face with a gun . . . is that you defending yourself?

The Jewish people have suffered so much. In Europe, in the Middle East. Shouldn't they be allowed their own home?

Of course they have, but you cannot replace one suffering with another and think the problem is solved. The State of Israel was formed through emptying 600 villages, ethnically displacing 750,000 Palestinians, and –

So what's the point of us being here?

It is about building solidarity where there is power. Here in Italy, in the West, there is power. It is about putting pressure on the Israelis.

But isn't –

It is exhausting.

At the end of a particularly antagonistic meeting, when it felt like the Italians would never understand, Janet turns to me and says:

Ily jai ahsan min ily ra-h.

(*Beat.*)

What is coming is better than what has gone.

Where did you learn this?

I have my ways.

//

Bilal   Border control at Tel Aviv airport have taken my passport. We're held up for an hour. They don't interrogate me as such, but they do take down my home address, telephone number and email. So, Netanyahu, if you do find my nudes, you're welcome boo!

The drive to Ramallah, where my Aunties live, takes about half an hour. The Aunties are Feya and Nada by the way, my grandad's sisters.

Their house is beautiful, made of limestone with these bright green iron doors that match the colour of the fig trees all around it.

The door opens, and Nada comes out.

(**Bilal** *signs: 'What's wrong? What happened?'*)

But she's pissed off.

(**Bilal** *signs: 'The Israelis pulled me in for questioning. We're sorry.'*)

She's pissed off that we're an hour late. She thought something had happened. The Aunties are both deaf and can't speak, by the way, so she's communicating all of this to us in our own family sign language.

But then we do start hugging and kissing. And they've obviously made us about a seven-course feast even though it is one in the morning. And after I've stuffed my face they rush us to bed because they have a whole day planned for us before the wedding.

//

Wa'el February 1968. The movement is growing all over the world for Palestine. We have new leaders, new organisations made up of actual Palestinians. Yasser Arafat, Ghassan Kanafani, George Habash, Hanna Mikhail.

And things really begin to change. In Italy you hear it in the coffee shops. Students reading Kanafani, smoking cigarettes and discussing liberation.

A year later, in 1969, Hanna Mikhail visits Milan.

And 20,000 Italians come to watch him speak.

20,000 Italians come to watch a Palestinian speak about Palestine.

When we go to watch Janet whispers in my ear:

Ily jai ahsan min ily ra-h.

//

Bilal   Sometimes when I speak to friends, well-meaning ones, progressives, whatever – they always say the same thing: the situation in Palestine is hopeless.

Last summer in London, when the violence kicked off, after the evictions in Sheikh Jarrah, and obviously after seventy years of brutal occupation and all that, 160,000 people took to the streets.

One hundred and sixty thousand.

160,000 is approximately the population size of Nablus, the town that Wa'el grew up in.

This isn't hopeless.

(*The chant 'Free, Free Palestine' is heard, and gets louder and louder. It blends with other sounds of the 2021 'Unity Intifada': Mohammed El-Kurd being interviewed, snippets of news bulletins, viral videos, major protests – including London's.*)

RECORDING:

Marwaan   But now we have hope. I don't know.

Bilal   Do you feel hopeful?

Marwaan   Hope [. . .] because the world is start looking at our problem from a different point of view.

//

(*A phone rings.* **Wa'el** *picks it up. He listens for a long time.*)

(*He hangs up, reluctant to speak.*)

Wa'el   The PFLP organise a shooting in Lod airport which kills twenty-eight people.

How does shooting civilians help our cause?

Cori has this strange smile on his face when I see him now, like he's telling me 'I told you so'.

Then, eleven Israeli Olympic Athletes are taken hostage and killed in Munich by a Palestinian group called Black September.

And less people start turning up to our meetings on Thursdays.

To the West the Palestinians become murderers or disorganised children, or both. And once again, we begin to lose that elusive commodity that we had given up everything for: sympathy.

Of course Israel responds. Responds like they always do, with disproportionate violence. And people are killed. Hundreds of Palestinians are killed.

Ghassan Kanafani. April 1972. My hero.

I write an obituary for him. But it's hard. How do you represent a life?

The mail we receive at the centre keeps getting scarier.

'*Do you not think they were justified in killing him?*'

'*Can you confirm if Kanafani was involved in the hijacking of aircraft carrier –*'

'*There is only one way to deal with an unruly beast – kill it.*'

My chest tightens with the weight of it. The letters, the media coverage, the killings, all of it –

It's only a month.

I know, and you should –

And it's a really important exhibition.

(*Beat.*)

Yes, you're right.

You're going to burn yourself out from all of this. Why don't you come with me?

To Sydney?

It's okay to take time away.

I have responsibilities, people here, the Committee, they rely on me.

I just wish you'd stop worrying so much.

I'm not choosing to feel like this, Janet –

You are choosing how to react to it. It's exhausting to be around you when –

Exhausting to be around me?

(*Beat.*)

When you're like this, yes.

Exhausting for you?

For both of us.

You're not the one getting those letters.

I never said tha –

You're not the one being threatened. The one struggling to sleep at night, how could you even –

I'm sorry that you're tired, but that's not –

You should be sorry for leaving.

(*Beat.*)

You're joking.

Leaving me at a time when –

This is my career, this is my whole –

Halas, get on the plane to your fancy exhibition.

You're being totally un –

Just remember please, when you're thousands of miles away, whose neck is on the line.

I have a life beyond you and your paranoia Wa'el –

YOU UNDERSTAND NOTHING!

And I storm off. And she goes to Sydney the next morning. And we don't speak.

There is so much rage. Everyone who looks at me. The world, who can turn on you within seconds. And I don't like feeling angry. I am not an angry person.

But it becomes harder to see people.

Amico, come out of your room!

Wa'el, I finished the last three pages of Sindbad . . . I'll leave it by your door.

Guaili . . . soup is cold . . . please come out.

And I just want to feel like a human being again.

And not an angry Palestinian.

//

(A record player plays 'Nour Balady', or a song with similar Arabic percussion.)

Wa'el I'm waiting alone for a Committee meeting.

It is twenty past eight. Still no-one. At least Leila or Salvatore should have arrived by now.

The mint tea has gone cold.

Eight-thirty. I take a look outside onto Via Mario. It is empty, except for two strangers laughing and holding hands.

Eight-forty. Finally someone comes in.

(*American accent.*) *Buongiorno, where is the Piazza Annibaliano?*

I can't speak. He looks at me strangely and leaves.

(*The music swells.*)

My body decides before my mind does: it's over, halas.

And I rip down the sign from the door.

(*He tears down the centre. He starts slowly, but soon the anger completely takes over in a way it never has before.*)

I destroy it all. I tear it all down. All of it.

(*The centre lies in tatters all around him.*)

The whole thing.

(*He goes to tear down the Palestinian flag, but just before he does –*)

Guaili.

Mariuccia's appeared in the doorway. The remains of the centre are . . .

Guaili.

I'm just tired, Mariuccia.

Do you know why I call you Guaili?

(**Mariuccia** *laughs.*)

And she's laughing. In the middle of all this chaos there is Mariuccia's laughter?

What's so funny?

I was so in love.

That's not what this is about –

He was so handsome . . . dio mio, the prettiest boy in village. Nice moustache. Not like you. Big. Thick. We call him Guaili because his voice so high . . . like singer. I was so in love.

Mariuccia this isn't about love, this is –

It's all love Guaili. It's always love.

//

Hello.

It's good to see you.

How long was the journey?

Long.

(*Pause.*)

I shouldn't have blamed you.

No.

You must be exhausted.

Yeah.

I'm so sorry.

I'm so tired.

(*Pause.*)

It's okay to stop.

You've never had anything to prove.

(*Beat.*)

Maybe for a while?

Maybe for a while.

Tell me about home. Please.

Janet talks all about Sydney and her family and the exhibition. We play music, and dance, and I feel something thaw, and I hope she feels it too.

(**Wa'el** *and* **Janet** *sway to the music.*)

I missed you.

I missed you too.

(*Blackout. The music fades.*)

//

(*The silence is broken by the sudden and loud sound of 'Dammi Falastini' playing.*)

(*We are at a Palestinian wedding: The glamour, the grandeur, the joy.*)

(**Bilal** *is dancing to his heart's content. Perhaps he tries to get a particularly keen audience member to join him.*)

Bilal   West Jerusalem. 8 September, 2018. It's Ahmed's wedding!

(*An uproar in the music.* **Bilal** *sings along: 'Go, go, go, go!'. He gets the audience to clap along with him. He's having the time of his life.*)

There must be about 200 people here.

And everyone is dancing!

(*For a moment, the music slows down, and* **Bilal** *comes to a stop.*)

And when Ahmed walks into the hall with Alaa, everything sort of stops for a moment. Alaa is wearing a white dress encrusted with these shimmering stones that keep catching the moonlight.

She looks iconic. Like a princess, straight out of the *1001 Nights*.

And Ahmed, oh Ahmed.

He's in a full-on tuxedo. With the shiniest black lace-ups. And his hair is slicked to one side – and in this moment I do cry. I cry because it's Ahmed, because it's his wedding.

And I do look like a Palestinian aunty, as he walks past me and I grab his cheek and

'Habibi!!!! Go, go, go, go!'

(*Uproar in music and* **Bilal** *starts dancing again.*)

I look in the middle of the circle and Feya and Nada are there too, dancing with each other.

I can't help but think how beautiful everyone here is. How joyful.

And then we sit down, and the food starts coming and it doesn't stop. We're talking shish ta'ok, falafel, labneh, tabouleh, fatoush. And you know the best bit?

Israeli waiters! We are being served by Israeli waiters. And my family are all like:

Sorry, this lemonade is not sweet enough, more sugar please.

I said tea with mint, not mint tea. Take it back.

Sorry, we asked for Palestinian hummus, not Israeli chickpea dip.

(*Nina Simone's rendition of 'Who Knows Where the Time Goes?' plays.*)

And Ahmad and Alaa dance arm in arm on the dancefloor, and everyone watches. And for a second I think this genuinely might be a dream, but then I feel a pinch on my shoulder.

It's Feya, and she takes me around the corner of the building. We can still hear the song.

(**Feya** *pulls out a packet of Marlboro Golds. She signs at* **Bilal** *to 'shh!' and lights the cigarette, taking a deep, satisfying drag. She hands the cigarette to* **Bilal**.)

She tells me that she doesn't want to smoke in front of the other aunties because they might gossip about her. I tell her that her secret is safe with me.

(**Bilal** *signs as he speaks the following:*)

And then she says she can't wait for my wedding. I say me neither, and that I hope it's as grand as this one. And she says it will be just as grand.

Because Hasnas are princes and princesses, she says. Kings and queens.

(*Silence. Calm. Joy – Palestinian joy.*)

Eventually we all bundle into the car and drive back to Ramallah. And we tumble into bed at 3am, completely spent, and completely happy.

//

(**Wa'el** *and* **Janet** *still dancing from before.*)

RECORDING:

Bilal   So you think we should put it in after the wedding?

Aaron   Yeah . . . yeah.

Bilal   Yeah . . .

Aaron   What do you think?

Bilal   I don't know. I just don't want it to be the last thing people see of him. You know?

Aaron   Yeah.

Wa'el   I want to write about love in the *1001 Nights*.

Well you should write it. But I'm going to sleep.

I'll be back before you wake up.

On my way home I stop at the shop to buy some wine and bread and I listen to Rome at night, smelling the shopkeepers' oranges mixed with the sweet summer breeze.

And I can't help feeling like I carry the music of Janet with me wherever I go.

(*He sways a bit like he did earlier.*)

As I turn onto Via Mario de Fiori, Mariuccia walks past and gives me a wink. What is she doing out so late?

I live, Guaili.

I get to Number 19 and walk down the corridor to the lift. It is occupied so I wait, but I don't mind waiting now.

I'm already formulating the article. There's too many ideas, but I don't have a pen on me.

So I wait and start writing in my head.

I want to use the *1001 Nights* to make a political argument about love.

And I wait.

(**Wa'el**'s *voice slowly turns into* **Bilal**'s.)

About how all causes for liberation are connected. How freedom cannot come in isolation or at the expense of another.

And I wait.

How if everything is connected then everything is vulnerable.

(*The elevator dings.*)

RECORDING:

Aaron It just feels like it would be – I don't know, it just feels like it would be weird if we don't put it in. Does that make sense?

Bilal   Yeah, it makes sense.

Aaron   Yeah?

Bilal   Maybe we could talk about the night before.

Aaron   Mmhm.

Bilal   And the article, and the bottle of wine, and the baguette.

Aaron   Yeah, yeah.

Bilal   And Janet, and the dance . . .

Aaron   Like him going home and stuff?

Bilal   Yeah.

Aaron   But do you agree?

Bilal   Yeah. I think we have to put it in.

//

(*All sense of artifice is stripped away now. We're all just in a room, talking.*)

Bilal   Wa'el was shot twelve times.

It was part of a series of assassinations by the Israeli government called 'Operation Wrath of God'.

He was carrying a bottle of red wine, a baguette, and his copy of the *1001 Nights*. They fired thirteen bullets. Twelve hit his body. The thirteenth was found lodged in Volume 2 of the *Nights*.

In the corner of an Italian paper the following day, a small headline read: 'Arab man killed in mystery attack'.

In the court hearing later that year, they declared Wa'el Zuaiter to be a 'Jordanian citizen'.

And that's really all I want to say about what happened.

Because I think I'm allowed to stop there.

(*Pause.*)

But surely you knew he was going to be killed?

Surely you expected it?

I mean, that's always the conclusion, isn't it?

Surely we wouldn't have gotten the funding to make the play unless he was killed?

Because what do Palestinians do except vanish, in one way or another?

RECORDING:

Bilal   Do you feel closer to Lebanon, or Palestine?

Hani   I feel closer to Lebanon, habibi, I don't know much about Palestine, I've just visited there. Lebanon I lived there, my friends were there.

Bilal   I never went for that cigarette with Feya by the way. I made that up.

I made it up because the Aunties never came to the wedding. They got turned away at the checkpoint.

The Aunties got turned away at the checkpoint because they were Palestinian and it was a Saturday. It was Shabbat so they were considered a terror threat.

The Aunties got turned away at the checkpoint because of settler colonialism and apartheid.

Because of the same system that killed Wa'el.

Because of America. Because of France. Egypt. Jordan. The UAE. Because of 1948 . . .

because of 1967 because of –

RECORDING:

Hani   'We must not forget about Britain.'

Bilal Because of BRITAIN.

Britain who colonised Palestine in 1920.

Britain who murdered thousands of Palestinians.

Britain who left their weapons to the terror groups who performed the Nakba.

Britain who still gives hundreds of millions –

RECORDING:

Hani Britain is a fantastic place, fantastic home. It's really looked after me, it's looked after mama, Bapu, Nani, everybody.

At the end of the day, Britain has been good to me. Britain is what shaped me, really. You know, Britain is what shaped me. I went to Britain when I was seventeen. Sometimes now, I'm more British than Arab.

(*Beat.*)

Bilal We still went. My mum, my dad, and I.

We didn't need to queue up at the checkpoint. We didn't need to walk through the cages and the turnstiles. We didn't need a pass, or a permit, or a visa, or a letter of approval. The Israeli soldiers treated us like we were celebrities.

Because *we* were British.

RECORDING:

Bilal If I ask you the question 'where am I from?', like Bilal, me, like where am I from? What would you say?

Hani It's difficult to put it all in one word or one sentence for you, Bilalu.

Bilal Sometimes I don't know if I'm Palestinian. I mean listen to me. I don't speak Arabic either, by the way – all the lines in this show I had to learn.

My dad wasn't even born in Palestine. His parents left just before the Nakba to try and start a life in Lebanon.

Sometimes I think all of this is me trying to prove to myself that I'm Palestinian.

(*Pause.*)

But there's this feeling.

And it really is impossible to translate.

But if you feel it you know what it is. If you're watching this and you're Palestinian, you know what it is.

It means you cry when you leave Palestine. And you cry at al Aqsa. And you cry when you watch the bombs falling over Gaza.

And it really is in your blood, and in your bones, and in your heart.

Wa'el spent his life keeping that feeling alive.

Because that feeling is love.

And it will never vanish.

It's all love. It's always love.

A few years after his murder, Janet contacted those who knew Wa'el. She wanted to help tell the story of his life.

Together with those friends, she compiled a series of essays from those closest to him about his life, about Palestine, about opera, and music, and the *1001 Nights*, and everything in between.

It's called 'For a Palestinian'.

(**Bilal** *shows the audience his copy of 'For A Palestinian'.*)

It was originally published in Italian, but they translated it into English as well, so more people in the West could read it.

There were only a few hundred copies published. But me and Aaron, who wrote this play with me, found a copy. It came from a place called Lyndhurst, New Jersey. It travelled 5,574 kilometres to get to us.

And it's the only reason we could tell the story of his life. Because someone chose to remember it. And now, all of us, in this room, know about it (with some creative licence).

And I don't want you to remember Wa'el just as someone who got assassinated.

Because Palestinians are so much more than their deaths.

I want you to remember Wa'el as someone who loved the smell of oranges and the taste of good Chianti.

As someone who started the Italian Committee in Support of the Palestinian People. Which still exists by the way.

As someone who had a sensitivity to the beauty of life in a way all of us could only dream of.

As someone who, above everything else, tried to translate this feeling.

RECORDING:

Bilal   Thank you so much Amo Marwan –

Marwaan   My pleasure Bilal . . . my pleasure . . . Yani, we need to keep all these stories for at least as you are doing – to write these stories in a way that the people of the world should know about it.

So I'm happy, I'm so happy that you asked me about this. And I'm so happy that you, you tried to make my memory alive again about that period of time. And I'm so happy that you know about what we went through during that time, because this is important. This is important for the Palestinian people to, to keep the memory of what happened and to take the lessons for the future. Which hopefully will be a good future for us Insha'Allah.

Bilal   Inshallah. Inshallah.

Bilal (*at the same time as the recording*)   Inshallah. Inshallah.

//

(**Bilal** *becomes* **Wa'el**. *Lighting, sound, performance. We're in a play again.*)

Wa'el   The message of the *1001 Nights* is simple, my albes: stories never finish.

We keep telling them in different ways, to different people, forever. And this is how it has always been, since the beginning of time.

It is the fabric of our beings, my dear.

And isn't this what love is, habibis and habibtis?

A story that never ends.

(*Blackout.*)

(*End of play.*)